EVERY STEP WITH JESUS

FOLLOWING THE SAINTS IN THE WAY OF THE CROSS

John Collins

www.osv.com
Our Sunday Visitor Publishing Division
Our Sunday Visitor, Inc.
Huntington, Indiana 46750

Scripture quotations are from the *Revised Standard Version of the Bible—Second Catholic Edition* (Ignatius Edition), copyright © 1965, 1966, 2006 National Council of the Churches of Christ in the United States of America. Used by permission. All rights reserved.

Every reasonable effort has been made to determine copyright holders of excerpted materials and to secure permissions as needed. If any copyrighted materials have been inadvertently used in this work without proper credit being given in one form or another, please notify Our Sunday Visitor in writing so that future printings of this work may be corrected accordingly.

Copyright © 2016 by Our Sunday Visitor Publishing Division, Our Sunday Visitor, Inc. Published 2016.

21 20 19 18 17 16   1 2 3 4 5 6 7 8 9

All rights reserved. With the exception of short excerpts for critical reviews, no part of this work may be reproduced or transmitted in any form or by any means whatsoever without permission from the publisher. For more information, visit: www.osv.com/permissions.

Our Sunday Visitor Publishing Division
Our Sunday Visitor, Inc.
200 Noll Plaza
Huntington, IN 46750
1-800-348-2440

ISBN: 978-1-68192-097-9 (Inventory No. T1832)
eISBN: 978-1-68192-108-2
LCCN: 2016952290

Cover design: Tyler Ottinger
Cover art: © Sedmak | Dreamstime.com
Interior design: Dianne Nelson

PRINTED IN THE UNITED STATES OF AMERICA

– ABOUT THE AUTHOR –

John Collins has been an editor for several prominent publishing companies including Doubleday, Dell, and St. Martin's Press. He began a long association with Father Benedict Groeschel during the 1990s when both of them worked to support the cause of canonization of Cardinal Terence Cooke. In 2008, John became Father Groeschel's personal editor, working closely with him on all his writings. He is the author of *A Friar's Tale: Remembering Fr. Benedict J. Groeschel, C.F.R.*

*Dedicated to the memory of
Father Benedict Joseph Groeschel,
who knew what it meant to walk
the Way of the Cross*

– CONTENTS –

– INTRODUCTION –
Walking with the Saints in
the Footsteps of Christ 8

– THE FIRST STATION –
Jesus Is Condemned to Death 11
St. John Paul II

– THE SECOND STATION –
Jesus Carries His Cross 17
St. Pio of Pietrelcina (Padre Pio)

– THE THIRD STATION –
Jesus Falls for the First Time 23
St. Thomas More

– THE FOURTH STATION –
Jesus Meets His Blessed Mother . . . 29
St. Bernard of Clairvaux

– THE FIFTH STATION –
Simon of Cyrene Helps
Jesus Carry His Cross 35
St. Leo the Great

– THE SIXTH STATION –
Veronica Wipes the Face of Jesus . . . 41
St. Thérèse of Lisieux

– THE SEVENTH STATION –
Jesus Falls for the Second Time 47
Dame Julian of Norwich

– THE EIGHTH STATION –
Jesus Meets the Women
of Jerusalem 53
St. John Chrysostom

– THE NINTH STATION –
Jesus Falls for the Third Time 59
St. Faustina

– THE TENTH STATION –
Jesus Is Stripped of His Garments . . . 65
St. Thomas Aquinas

– THE ELEVENTH STATION –
Jesus Is Nailed to the Cross 71
   St. Cyril of Jerusalem

– THE TWELFTH STATION –
Jesus Dies on the Cross 75
   St. Augustine

– THE THIRTEENTH STATION –
Jesus Is Taken Down
from the Cross 79
   St. Catherine of Siena

– THE FOURTEENTH STATION –
Jesus Is Laid in the Tomb 85
   St. Teresa of Calcutta

– THE FIFTEENTH STATION –
The Resurrection 91
   St. Teresa Benedicta of the Cross (Edith Stein)

– INTRODUCTION –

Walking with the Saints in the Footsteps of Christ

"Out of darkness is born the light," writes St. Catherine of Siena. And in those few words she offers us a gift: a perfect way to begin our mediation on the Way of the Cross. Yet the birth of light is rarely on our minds as we follow Jesus' slow and painful climb to Golgotha's heights, for the darkness is too apparent, the gathering gloom too great. The light that Catherine perceives hides from us. We know it will come on Easter morning, but on Good Friday doesn't darkness reign supreme?

Catherine and the other saints are emphatic in their answer: No it does not! How could it, for the Way of the Cross is the way to the Resurrection, the way of redemption? The saints tell us that this dark journey contains within itself a great and powerful light that is present from the beginning, but is not apparent until the end. Long before Jesus stands in front of Pilate, the light of a new dawn has become real. It shines within Him and from His every act. It shines forth from the divine will that gives us a Savior and allows Him to live and die as one of us. It is a light powerfully present in every step Jesus takes as He makes His way through a darkness that becomes light, to a death that becomes life.

Catherine of Siena knows that "out of darkness is born the light," just as she knows that out of Jesus' sorrowful death unconquerable life is born. This is not just her vision but also the vision of countless saints who preceded us. We look to them as they lead us from Pilate's unjust court to the brilliance of Easter morning. We meditate on their words and allow those words to dispel the darkness that surrounds us — that pervades us. With their help we begin to perceive the light concealed within darkness and to accept the cross as the tree of unending life. Perhaps this understanding is captured most perfectly by St. Theodore the Studite, a monk whose life straddled the eighth and ninth centuries. So we will linger for a moment on his words before we begin to walk with Our Savior to His death … and to our life:

> How precious the gift of the cross,
> how splendid to contemplate!
> In the cross there is no mingling
> of good and evil, as in the tree
> of paradise: it is wholly beautiful
> to behold and good to taste. The
> fruit of this tree is not death but
> life, not darkness but light. This
> tree does not cast us out of paradise, but opens the way for our
> return. (Quoted in the Office of
> Readings for the Second Week of
> Easter)

✝

– THE FIRST STATION –

Jesus Is Condemned to Death

St. John Paul II

The future Pope John Paul II was born Karol Jósef Wojtyła in Poland during the spring of 1920. His early life was far from ideal: He lost his mother and brother while still a child, and less than a decade later his father died as well. During World War II, Karol was forced by the Nazi occupation to abandon his studies and undertake backbreaking work in a quarry. Undaunted, he enrolled in an underground seminary and was ordained after the war.

The young priest became a seminary professor and then a bishop who participated in the Second Vatican Council. Named archbishop of Kraków in 1964 and a cardinal in 1967, he was involved in the writing of the famous encyclical *Humanae Vitae* ("Of Human Life"). In 1978, Cardinal Wojtyła was elected the first non-Italian pope in four centuries, embarking on a papacy that lasted nearly twenty-seven years. Pope John Paul II not only championed Christ and His Church in a world beset by secularism, atheism, and relativism, but he played a major role in the fall of communism. Perhaps the greatest of modern popes, St. John Paul II died in 2005 and was canonized in 2014. His feast day is October 22.

> **V.** We adore You, O Christ, and we praise You.
> **R.** Because by Your holy Cross You have redeemed the world.

– The First Station –

"And Pilate … said to them, 'Then what shall I do with the man whom you call the King of the Jews?' And they cried out again, 'Crucify him.' And Pilate said to them, 'Why, what evil has he done?' But they shouted all the more, 'Crucify him.' So Pilate, wishing to satisfy the crowd, released for them Barabbas; and having scourged Jesus, he delivered him to be crucified" (Mk 15:12-14).

A civil official discards truth. He makes his judgment based solely on expediency — choosing death because it has become more convenient than life. Thus the creature grasps at the power that belongs to the Creator alone. It has been decreed: blind, uncaring man, so enamored of destruction, will attempt to annihilate the source of his own being. The Son of God will be put to death by those He has come to save. What greater decision for death — for nothingness — can there be than Pilate's?

St. John Paul II knows this verdict to be a judgment on us all. Yet he also knows it to be the unavoidable first step on a path that leads not just to death but *through* it to life and the salvation for which we all yearn:

> God created man as rational and free, thereby placing himself under man's judgment. The history of salvation is also the history of man's continual judgment of God....
>
> This is the definitive meaning of Good Friday: Man, you who judge God, who order Him to justify himself before your tribunal, think about yourself, [think whether] you are not responsible for the death of this condemned man, [whether] the judgment of God is not actually a judgment

upon yourself. Consider if this judgment and its result — the Cross and then the Resurrection — are not your only way to salvation. (*Crossing the Threshold of Hope*)

Prayer

My Jesus, You are the innocent lamb, the One in whom no wrong can be found. Yet Pilate and countless others condemn You. Help me to see that no condemnation from sinful man can ever overcome the love You extend even to those who judge You. Grant me the grace to trust in Your ways. Never let me doubt You or judge the manner in which You choose to work in my life. Lord Jesus, never permit me to condemn You as Pilate did … as so many still do. Amen.

✝

– THE SECOND STATION –

Jesus Carries His Cross

St. Pio of Pietrelcina (Padre Pio)

Francesco Forgione, born in 1887 to a peasant family in southern Italy, displayed a devout faith from childhood. As a boy he yearned to join the Capuchin Franciscans, but did not have sufficient education to apply. So his father sailed to America where he earned the money to send his son to school. By the age of fifteen, Francesco was able to realize his dream: He took the Capuchin habit and the name of Pio. In 1918, Padre Pio underwent various mystical experiences, which were to continue for the rest of his life. These included the stigmata (the wounds of Christ), which he bore for five decades. An extraordinary priest, he heard confessions for up to twelve hours a day and was able to see into people's hearts more clearly than they could themselves. The miraculous seemed to surround him, resulting in Padre Pio having countless followers, but his detractors were numerous as well. He came under baseless attacks but endured them patiently. In 1968, his stigmata mysteriously healed itself — one month before his death. Padre Pio was canonized in 2002, and his feast day is September 23.

V. We adore You, O Christ, and we praise You.

R. Because by Your holy Cross You have redeemed the world.

– The Second Station –

"So they took Jesus, and he went out, bearing his own cross, to the place called the place of a skull, which is called in Hebrew Golgotha" (Jn 19:17).

Imagine the horror of not only being sentenced to a painful and lingering death but also of being presented with the instrument of your destruction as if it were a gift. What must it be like to have that "gift" placed upon your shoulders, a crushing burden that you must carry to the very place of your execution? Such treatment is so extreme that we are tempted to call it "inhuman" — except that we know it's *all too human*. Perhaps we can see nothing but darkness as Christ shoulders His cross and takes His first halting steps toward Golgotha. The light seems very far off, indeed. But St. Pio of Pietrelcina tells us otherwise: the journey to Golgotha is for him a procession to joy; it is the way to peace:

We must keep the eye of faith fixed on Jesus Christ who climbs the hill of Calvary loaded with His Cross, and as He toils painfully up the steep slope of Golgotha we should see Him followed by an immense throng of souls carrying their own crosses and treading the same path. Oh, what a beautiful sight this is. Let us fix our mental gaze firmly on it. We see close behind Jesus our most holy Mother, who follows Him perfectly, loaded with her own cross. Then comes the Apostles, Martyrs, Doctors, Virgins, and Confessors.... Jesus himself, despite all our unworthiness, has associated us with this beautiful company. We must make every effort to merge ourselves increasingly in these ranks and hasten with them along the road to Calvary. We should look to the end

– The Second Station –

of the journey and not separate ourselves from this fine company; we must refuse to follow any other way than the one they tread. (*Letters Volume III: Correspondence with His Spiritual Daughters [1915-23]*)

Prayer

My Jesus, I tremble at the thought of what You endured for me, and I tremble at the thought of the cross You may ask me to carry. Give me the grace to put aside my fears and doubts, to shoulder my cross and walk in Your footsteps and the footsteps of all the saints. Let me be part of that sacred company, as You lead us all from darkness into the Father's light. Amen.

†

– THE THIRD STATION –

Jesus Falls for the First Time

St. Thomas More

St. Thomas More was not simply a lawyer, writer, and statesman, but was also an influential Renaissance figure. A man of great intellectual ability, he entered Oxford University at fourteen and excelled at his studies. More was also a man of profound faith who yearned for the monastic life, although he ultimately remained a layman. Entering the political world, he rose quickly in the government of King Henry VIII, becoming Lord Chancellor, the highest position in England except for the king himself.

More served until Henry, eager for a divorce that the pope would never grant him, declared himself head of the Church in England. More resigned his office. Yet Henry demanded that all people of influence sign an oath accepting the crown's royal supremacy over the Church. While almost all the bishops and clergy in England submitted, More refused. He was imprisoned in the Tower of London, where he spent his time contemplating Christ's passion. Thomas More was beheaded on July 6, 1535. He was canonized in 1935, and his feast day is June 22.

> V. We adore You, O Christ, and
> we praise You.
> R. Because by Your holy Cross
> You have redeemed the world.

– The Third Station –

"Surely he has borne our griefs / and carried our sorrows; / yet we esteemed him stricken, / struck down by God, and afflicted" (Is 53:4).

The incarnate Savior does not wear our frail humanity as a garment but makes it part of himself. And He permits His humanity to be pushed beyond all limits — pushed so far that He no longer possesses even the strength to resist gravity's gentle pull. As His steps falter, He falls heavily, painfully. Is it at this moment — as we contemplate Him prone, gasping, pinned down by the cross — that we finally see that Jesus is one of us? Is it at this moment that we realize how perfectly He has subsumed His power in our weakness? Our exhaustion has become God's exhaustion; our fear has become God's fear. His falling to the ground is our inevitable falling into death. Jesus falls on the harsh road to Golgotha so that we may rise with Him. St. Thomas More sees the battered humanity of the fallen Christ, but he also knows that tormented figure to be the divine bearer of eternal victory:

> As for our Savior Christ, what happened ... showed how far He was from letting His sadness, fear, and weariness prevent Him from obeying His Father's command and keep Him from carrying out with courage all those things which He had formerly regarded with wise and wholesome fear. For the time being, however, He had more than one reason why He should choose to suffer fear, sadness, weariness, and grief — "choose" I say, not "be forced," for who could have forced God? Quite the contrary, it was by His own marvelous arrangement that

– The Third Station –

His divinity moderated its influence on His humanity for such a time and in such a way that He was able to yield to the passions of our frail humanity and to suffer them with such terrible intensity....

For though His divinity is equal and identical to that of God the Father, nevertheless because He is also man He casts himself down humbly as a man, face down on the earth before God the Father. (*The Sadness of Christ*)

Prayer

My Jesus, I watch as You walk the road to death. I see each labored breath become a torture, each step an agony. Before my eyes Your strength deserts You until You cannot stand. You fall on hard stone, as I would fall, for no angel swoops down to catch You and hold You gently. You lie beneath the weight of the cross, but I know it is really the weight of my sins that pins You to the earth. Forgive me, Lord Jesus. Give me the strength to sin no more. Never let me add anything to the weight You bear for me. Amen.

†

– THE FOURTH STATION –

Jesus Meets His Blessed Mother

St. Bernard of Clairvaux

St. Bernard of Clairvaux was born in France in 1090. At the age of twenty, along with a group of relatives and friends, he entered the monastery at Citeaux, reviving the nearly moribund institution so completely that it was able to establish a new house in a place named Clairvaux. Bernard became abbot there, and in his nearly four-decade-long tenure founded sixty-five new monasteries. A negotiator of rare ability, he successfully ended the papal schism of the twelfth century, which had begun with the election of an antipope named Anacletus II. Idealistically, Bernard encouraged the Second Crusade, and his influence was so powerful that large armies from all across Europe marched to the Middle East to liberate the Holy Land. Attacks on Jews in the Rhineland brought Bernard to Germany in a successful effort to end the persecution. A theologian so profound that he was called "the last of the Fathers," Bernard has left us many writings that are avidly studied today. He died in 1153 and was canonized in 1174. One of the Doctors of the Church, his feast day is August 20.

> V. We adore You, O Christ, and we praise You.
> R. Because by Your holy Cross You have redeemed the world.

– The Fourth Station –

"But standing by the cross of Jesus were his mother, and his mother's sister, Mary the wife of Clopas, and Mary Magdalene" (Jn 19:25).

A mother loves her child in ways too deep to comprehend, too strong to fade. Maternal love is a reflection of divine love; unlocking heaven's gate, it allows new life to enter the world. Yet such love carries a risk almost too great to bear: In our fallen world a love too strong to fade can give birth to a grief too intense to end. Imagine a mother watching her child die in agony. Surely something within her dies as well. She may continue to live, but hers is a life devoured by grief. Our Blessed Mother forces herself through the crowd in an anguished attempt to comfort her Son. When she looks into Jesus' eyes she discovers in them the pain of the whole world. With what can she counter such pain? She has nothing — nothing but a mother's love. Mary's closeness to God is beyond our grasping, but St. Bernard of Clairvaux knows that it offers her no protection on Good Friday. He knows her suffering is white-hot because that is the intensity of her love:

> Perhaps someone will say: "Had she not known before that he would not die?" Undoubtedly. "Did she not expect him to rise again at once?" Surely. "And still she grieved over her crucified Son?" Intensely. Who are you and what is the source of your wisdom that you are more surprised at the compassion of Mary than at the passion of Mary's Son? For if he could die in body, could she not die with him in spirit? He died in body through a love greater than anyone had known. She died in spirit through a love

– The Fourth Station –

unlike any other since his. (From a Sermon by St. Bernard, found in the Office of Readings)

Prayer

My Jesus, when You meet Your mother on the road to Golgotha You meet the one whose love for You is purest. I know I cannot love You as she does, but I ask You to grant me the grace to love You with all my strength. Give me the ability to see You in everyone who suffers, to offer what I can to soothe their pain. Permit me to become like Your holy Mother, to love greatly, even when love opens the gates of sorrow. Amen.

†

– THE FIFTH STATION –

Simon of Cyrene Helps
Jesus Carry His Cross

St. Leo the Great

St. Leo the Great, son of an aristocratic Tuscan family, became pope in 440, a period during which the Roman Empire was disintegrating and the Church was beset by many problems. For twenty-one years he fought against numerous heresies, including Monophysitism (the belief that Christ had only a divine nature) and Nestorianism (the belief that two distinct natures exist in Christ — one divine, one human). Theological problems, however, were far from the only issues Pope Leo faced. In 452, fierce barbarian tribes called Huns threatened Rome. Leo met with Attila, their leader, in an effort to save the city. The pope prevailed and Rome was left untouched. Only three years later, though, Leo was face to face with the leader of another attacking horde. The Vandals were at the gates of Rome this time. Leo met with their leader, and again the attackers retreated. Leo the Great is numbered among the Doctors of the Church and has left many letters and sermons of great depth. He died in 461, and his feast day is November 10.

> V. We adore You, O Christ, and we praise You.
>
> R. Because by Your holy Cross You have redeemed the world.

– The Fifth Station – 37

"As they were marching out, they came upon a man of Cyrene, Simon by name; this man they compelled to carry his cross" (Mt 27:32).

Simon is anything but a volunteer. The Romans press him into service, and what a horrible service it is — taking part in the execution of someone he doesn't even know. Cyrene is on the North African coast, and from it Simon journeys to the "city of peace" to be forced to participate in this horrible torture. Imagine how confused he must have been that day in Jerusalem. Does he even know of what Jesus had been convicted? Who can say? But we do know that when Simon lifts the cross, he gives relief to a man in torment. In following the executioners' demands he helps Jesus more than do any of the Savior's followers. We are so much like Simon — confused, unaware, frightened, often forced to do things we don't want to do. Sometimes we can't even tell good from bad. But like Simon of Cyrene, if we pick up the cross and walk with Jesus, we will accomplish things of greater depth and meaning than we can imagine. St. Leo the Great sees in Simon's carrying of the cross a symbol of the glory that the Cross of Christ offers to us — offers to the entire world:

> But as the multitudes went with Jesus to the place of punishment, a certain Simon of Cyrene was found on whom to lay the wood of the cross, instead of the Lord. Even this act signified that faith would come to the Gentiles, to whom the cross of Christ was not to be shame but glory. It was not accidental therefore but symbolic and mystical, that while the Jewish rulers were raging against Christ, a foreigner was found to share his sufferings. Thus the apostle would

– The Fifth Station –

say, "If we suffer with him, we shall also reign with him." (Sermon LIX, cited in *Ancient Christian Commentary on Scripture: New Testament Ib, Matthew 14-28*)

Prayer

My Jesus, Your great burden has been eased by a man from a faraway country, a man who doesn't even know You. Give me the grace to be like Simon of Cyrene. Permit me to carry the crosses of those who suffer, even if only for a moment — even if they are strangers to me — for it is in lifting the pain of others that the sorrow of the Cross is transformed into glory. Amen.

✝

– THE SIXTH STATION –

Veronica Wipes the Face of Jesus

St. Thérèse of Lisieux

In 1873, Thérèse was born to a family not only of faith but also of real holiness. Her parents were canonized in 2015, and her four sisters preceded her into the cloister. Yet her early life was a mixture of darkness and light. Her mother, Zélie, died when Thérèse was four years old, which led the young girl to become withdrawn. Pauline, her eldest sister, entered the Carmelite monastery when Thérèse was still very young, leaving the little girl feeling that she'd lost a mother twice. Yet on Christmas Eve 1886, Thérèse's melancholy evaporated. Determined to give herself to Christ, she entered Carmel at the age of sixteen and spent the rest of her life — a mere nine years — there. At twenty-two she exhibited signs of tuberculosis, the disease that would take her life. She underwent great suffering and the temptation to despair, but she triumphed and died in Christ's loving embrace.

Her memoir, *The Story of a Soul*, has a spiritual profundity that seems impossible for one so young. Thérèse died at the age of twenty-four on September 30, 1897. She was canonized in 1925 and declared a Doctor of the Church in 1997. Her feast day is October 1.

> V. We adore You, O Christ, and we praise You.

– The Sixth Station –

R. Because by Your holy Cross
You have redeemed the world.

"He has delivered us from the dominion of darkness and transferred us to the kingdom of his beloved Son, in whom we have redemption, the forgiveness of sins. He is the image of the invisible God, the first-born of all creation" (Col 1:13-15).

Jesus suffered many blows on the road to Golgotha, surrounded as He was by those who reached out their hands to inflict pain. Only one person used her hands to soothe: the woman we call Veronica. Imagine the courage it took to push through the crowd, to wipe Jesus' bloody face right in front of those who were screaming for His death. The sole instance of physical kindness found in the Way of the Cross, Veronica's act of compassion is a bright island in a sea of cruelty. Perhaps it seems small when balanced against the unrelenting brutality of that day. But small things can be important. After wiping Jesus' face, Veronica's veil should have been stained with dirt and blood. Instead it bore the image of the Savior.

St. Thérèse, who sought heaven doing little things, finds a revelation in Veronica's "little" act, unveiling the Son of God:

> Remember that a Condemned Man,
> Overwhelmed with suffering, turning to Heaven,
> Cried out, "Soon you will see me Appear glorious in power."
> No one wanted to believe that He was the Son of God,
> For His ineffable glory was hidden …
> O Prince of Peace,
> As for me, I recognize you,
> I believe in You!…

– The Sixth Station –

Remember that your divine Face
Was always unknown to your own people;
But you left your sweet image for me,
And you know it well, I *did* recognize you …
Yes, I know you, all veiled in tears.
Face of the Eternal One, I discover your charms
Jesus, all the hearts
Who gather your tears
Remember.
(From "Jesus My Beloved, Remember" in *The Poetry of Saint Thérèse of Lisieux*)

Prayer

My Jesus, Your suffering scorches my soul. Yet I do not move forward to wipe the sweat from Your face or clean away the dirt and blood that disfigure You. I offer you no drop of water, nor do I help carry the cross that burdens You. Instead, fearful, I wait with the crowd, watching a woman struggle forward. She touches Your face with her veil, and her veil unveils the dawn. Give me the strength to be like the woman who comforts You. Let me do whatever I can for all who walk the Way of the Cross — for You. Amen.

✝

– THE SEVENTH STATION –

Jesus Falls for the Second Time

Dame Julian of Norwich

Julian of Norwich is a mysterious figure. Little is known of her life, yet her mystical writings are profound. Even her name is uncertain; we call her "Julian" because she was an anchoress (a woman who withdraws from the world to live a life of solitude and prayer) at the Church of St. Julian in Norwich. She was born in 1342 and at the age of thirty was stricken with an illness that brought her to the point of death. A priest was called to administer the last rites. He held a crucifix over her, and Julian saw the figure on it begin to bleed. This began a series of mystical visions that continued as Julian lay in bed. When the visions ended five days later, she had recovered — and been transformed. Julian wrote an account of her experiences, which she called "Showings." Entitled *Revelations of Divine Love*, it has been studied ever since. Although Julian has never been officially canonized, many are devoted to her. They observe May 8 or May 13 as her feast day, since it was between those dates that she experienced her visions.

> **V.** We adore You, O Christ, and we praise You.
> **R.** Because by Your holy Cross You have redeemed the world.

– The Seventh Station –

"Take my yoke upon you, and learn from me; for I am gentle and lowly in heart, and you will find rest for your souls" (Mt 11:29).

Jesus grows weaker with each step. Yet He struggles on, His every muscle screaming in agony. He can barely stand. Yet, still, He inches forward, bowed down beneath the weight of the cross. Finally, His legs buckle, and He collapses again. How can God permit such torment? How can a loving Father permit *any torment at all*? In the Way of the Cross we are starkly confronted not just with the reality of suffering but the necessity of it — confronted with something we can neither comprehend nor avoid. As we watch the agonized Jesus fall a second time, all we can do is accept what the Way of the Cross teaches: that hidden within suffering is the mysterious path to redemption.

Despite her mystical visions, Julian of Norwich understands the mystery of suffering no better than we do, but she doesn't care. As we see from the three short quotations below she is too focused on the God whose love transforms everything to worry about suffering at all:

> If there is anywhere on earth a lover of God is always kept safe, I know nothing of it, for it was not shown to me. But this was shown: that in falling and rising again we are always kept in that same precious love.

> We need to fall, and we need to be aware of it; for if we did not fall, we should not know how weak and wretched we are of ourselves, nor should we know

– The Seventh Station –

our Maker's marvelous love so fully.

See that I am God. See that I am in everything. See that I do everything. See that I have never stopped ordering my works, nor ever shall, eternally. See that I lead everything on to the conclusion I ordained for it before time began, by the same power, wisdom, and love with which I made it. How can anything be amiss? (Each quotation from *Revelations of Divine Love*)

Prayer

Lord Jesus, I do not understand why You fall to the ground for me, why Your suffering is so necessary for my joy. But I thank

You for all that Your cross has won for me. Teach me to accept that the path ahead might be filled with difficulties and pain. Never let me forget that the Father orders all things, that He loves me, and that He will give me the strength to rise no matter how many times I fall. Amen.

†

– THE EIGHTH STATION –

Jesus Meets the Women of Jerusalem

St. John Chrysostom

John Chrysostom means "John the golden-mouthed," for this saint was a man of unusual eloquence, someone who was able to express the truths of the Church in the most beautiful and penetrating ways. Born in Antioch about 349, he felt the pull of Christ at an early age and retired to the wilderness to lead a life of prayer, penance, and contemplation. Frail health, however, eventually forced him back to the city, where he was ordained to the diaconate and then the priesthood. John Chrysostom quickly became a powerful and beloved preacher, who attracted large crowds. In 397, he was named bishop of Constantinople. There he antagonized the aristocracy by his insistence on simplicity and asceticism, yet the common people loved him. A victim of political intrigue, Chrysostom was forced into exile despite the pope's clear support for him. St. John Chrysostom died far from home on September 14, 407. It is said that his final words were, "Glory be to God for all things." The feast day of this great Father and Doctor of the Church is September 13.

> V. We adore You, O Christ, and
> we praise You.
> R. Because by Your holy Cross
> You have redeemed the world.

– The Eighth Station –

"And there followed him a great multitude of the people, and of women who bewailed and lamented him. But Jesus turning to them said, 'Daughters of Jerusalem, do not weep for me, but weep for yourselves and for your children'" (Lk 23:27-28).

Who are these women who follow Jesus to Golgotha, who seem to want to help or are at least unwilling to let Him approach death alone? We know them only as the women of Jerusalem, but He must have known their names. Perhaps among them were the mothers and sisters of His apostles, the wives and daughters of friends. Maybe some were simply women who had watched Him from afar and had seen something unusual in a young iterant rabbi. Whoever they were, like Veronica, and Our Lady at the foot of the cross, these were women of compassion and courage. As they support Jesus they publically side with a criminal whom both the state and religious leaders have condemned. These women court danger — a danger they disregard. Peter disowns Jesus; almost all the apostles flee in terror. But the women walk with Him. They are exactly what we are called to be. They are what so few of us ever become. St. John Chrysostom is filled with admiration for the women of Jerusalem. He sees them as a light in the darkness and urges us all to follow them:

> Certain women were notably present as these things occurred. They were most inclined to feel for him, to grieve over his sufferings. Note how great is their constancy. They had followed him, ministering to him wherever he went. They were present even to the time of the dangers. They had seen all these events — how

– The Eighth Station –

he wept, how he yielded up his spirit....

These women were first to be attentive to Jesus at his death and burial. The sex most likely to be disparaged was first to enjoy the sight of his resurrected blessings. They most steadily showed their courage. Even when the disciples had fled in the darkness, these women were still present....

Let us men imitate these women! Let us not forsake Jesus in times of trial! These women exposed their lives so much for him even when he was dead, even as they had spent so much for him when he was alive. But we men, I repeat, neither feed him when hungry nor clothe him when naked. Seeing him begging, we pass by. And yet if we might really behold him in the neighbor, we would divest ourselves of all our goods. (From *Homily on the Gospel of Matthew 88.2-3*)

Prayer

My Jesus, I love You but do not walk with You. I fear the strident voices of the world that jeer at those who call themselves Your own. When I confess Your name my voice is a whisper that quickly fades away. Give me the grace to become like the women of Jerusalem and follow You to Golgotha and beyond. Give me the grace to stand with Your holy mother beneath the cross, to offer You the little I have as You offer everything for me. Amen.

✝

– THE NINTH STATION –

Jesus Falls for the Third Time

St. Faustina

Born in Poland in 1905, Helen Kowalska experienced such awareness of Christ that she actually *saw* Him. This convinced her to become a religious, and she applied to many communities, all of which rejected her until the Sisters of Our Lady of Mercy finally agreed to admit her — if she provided her own habit. Working as a maid to earn the money, Helen soon achieved her dream, taking as her religious name Sister

Maria Faustina of the Most Blessed Sacrament. She lived an ordinary life until she experienced another vision of Jesus after an illness. He told her to have a picture painted exactly as she saw Him, and this is the picture of the Divine Mercy which hangs in Catholic churches today. Her visions of the Divine Mercy multiplied, and she recorded them in a diary that is among the most read spiritual books of our time. St. Faustina died at the age of thirty-three in 1938, was canonized in 2000, and her feast day is October 5. The Church now celebrates Divine Mercy Sunday a week after Easter. This feast is St. Faustina's gift to us.

> V. We adore You, O Christ, and we praise You.
> R. Because by Your holy Cross You have redeemed the world.

*"The steps of a man are from the L*ORD*, / and he establishes him in whose way he delights, /*

though he fall, he shall not be cast headlong, / for the LORD *is the stay of his hand" (Ps 37:23-24).*

Golgotha's crest comes into view. The place of death is but a short distance away. Does the One who has already suffered so much feel relief as He arrives at this awful place? Has He been so reduced that He yearns for nothing but an end to pain? Does He want to run to His death simply to get it over with? No matter: He can hardly walk. The road beneath His feet almost calls to Jesus. "Fall," it seems to say. "I will catch You, and You can rest on me. Fall as Lucifer fell, like a star from heaven. Fall as Adam fell from bliss into pain. Fall as Your torturers fell, deep into sin. Fall and never rise again." And Jesus does fall heavily onto the ground. He battles to regain his footing, using the last atoms of His strength. Finally, He is upright. Holding tightly to His cross, He steps toward His death — and toward our life.

St. Faustina sees two very different ways of falling on the road to Golgotha: the way the world falls — careless and unaware — and the way Christ falls — full of self-giving and purpose. She knows it is only the latter kind of fall from which it is possible to rise again:

> I saw two roads. One was broad, covered with sand and flowers, full of joy, music and all sorts of pleasures. People walked along it, dancing and enjoying themselves. They reached the end of the road without realizing it. And at the end of the road there was a horrible precipice; that is, the abyss of hell. The souls fell blindly into it; as they walked, so they fell. And their numbers were so great that it was impossible to count them. And I saw the other road,

– The Ninth Station –

or rather, a path, for it was narrow and strewn with thorns and rocks; and the people who walked along it had tears in their eyes, and all kinds of suffering befell them. Some fell down upon the rocks, but stood up immediately and went on. At the end of the road there was a magnificent garden filled with all sorts of happiness, and all these souls entered there. At the very first instant they forgot all their sufferings. (*Diary of Saint Maria Faustina Kowalska*)

Prayer

My Jesus, You carried more than Your cross as You struggled up the road to Golgotha. You carried me and my many sins. You held me tenderly every step of the way even though Your strength was failing and Your anguish growing. When You fell You protected me rather than yourself. Give me the grace to choose the path to Golgotha over the road of passing joy. Let me never fall into sin, and if I should fall, let me rise again with You. Amen.

†

– THE TENTH STATION –

Jesus Is Stripped of His Garments

St. Thomas Aquinas

St. Thomas Aquinas is among the Church's greatest theologians and the world's greatest philosophers. Born in Italy about 1225, he came from a well-to-do family and at the age of nineteen wanted to enter the Dominican order. His parents opposed this so strongly that they held Thomas prisoner for a year. The young man's determination, however, was such that his family relented, and he donned the habit of St. Dominic.

Thomas studied with the finest scholars of his time and by 1265 was so highly thought of that he served as papal theologian. Soon he produced the most famous of his many theological works, his *Summa Theologiae*. Thomas was twice regent master at the University of Paris, one of the major intellectual centers of Europe, and he wrote many brilliant theological treatises. In 1273, he underwent a mystical experience before an icon of Christ. Afterward he declined to write anything further. Perhaps the greatest theologian of all time said that what he experienced in that moment of ecstasy made all that he had written seem "like straw." Thomas Aquinas died on March 7, 1274, was canonized in 1323, and was declared a Doctor of the Church in 1567. His feast day is January 28.

V. We adore You, O Christ, and we praise You.

– The Tenth Station –

R. Because by Your holy Cross
You have redeemed the world.

"When the soldiers had crucified Jesus they took his garments and made four parts, one for each soldier; also his tunic. But the tunic was without seam, woven from top to bottom; so they said to one another, 'Let us not tear it, but cast lots for it to see whose it shall be'" (Jn 19:23-24).

To be crucified is not only to suffer unimaginable pain; it is to have everything ripped away — to be left with nothing. What shred of dignity — or even humanity — could cling to one who arrives, as Jesus does, battered and bloody, at Golgotha's peak? He comes at last to the place where He will lay down His cross, having carried it far longer than seemed possible. Soon it will carry Him, and it will do its work well, transporting Him from our loveless world to His loving Father. Yet Jesus is not yet completely bereft: He has His clothes.

Filthy and blood soaked, they are little enough, yet Roman soldiers tear them from Him, leaving Him naked before the gawking crowd. Having lost everything, Jesus becomes nothing to these men — less than the worn pieces of cloth at which they grasp. As Jesus touches the depths of our poverty, we know a moment of terror, for in His naked helplessness we see our own. Even now He retains His unity with the Father and so really lacks nothing. But what of us? The things of the world cannot save us. Do we know where our real hope lies? St. Thomas Aquinas teaches us to follow Jesus' example and cast off the passing things of this world to embrace treasures that can never be taken from us:

> If you seek an example of despising earthly things, follow him
> who is the King of kings and the
> Lord of lords, in whom are hidden

– The Tenth Station –

all the treasures of wisdom and knowledge. Upon the cross he was stripped, mocked, spat upon, struck, crowned with thorns, and given only vinegar and gall to drink.

Do not be attached, therefore, to clothing and riches, because "they divided my garments among themselves." Nor to honors, for he experienced harsh words and scourgings. Nor to greatness of rank, for "weaving a crown of thorns they placed it on my head." Nor to anything delightful, for "in my thirst they gave me vinegar to drink." (From a conference by St. Thomas Aquinas [*Collatio 6 super Credo in Deum*] presented in the Office of Readings)

Prayer

My Jesus, we enter this world with nothing, and with nothing we depart from it. The things that delight and divert us — the things at which we grasp — are but a handful of dust. In Bethlehem You took our poverty upon yourself, and on Golgotha You held fast to it. Grant me the grace to search for riches not in the emptiness prized by the world but in You alone. Permit me to lay down the things of this passing world and hold tight to the things of heaven. Amen.

†

– THE ELEVENTH STATION –

Jesus Is Nailed to the Cross

St. Cyril of Jerusalem

St. Cyril, who lived from about 313 to 386, is ranked among the Fathers of the Church and for about thirty-five tumultuous years he served as bishop of Jerusalem. For most of his life the Church was painfully divided by the Arian heresy, which emphatically denied the divinity of Christ. Cyril bravely resisted this heresy at a time when many Christians around him had succumbed to it. For his efforts he was exiled from his see on several occasions.

Cyril, however, never gave up and lived to see the Church vanquish the heresy that had cost him so much. A profound theologian, Cyril left behind significant writings, especially concerning catechesis and the liturgy. The Church celebrates his feast day on March 18.

- V. We adore You, O Christ, and we praise You.
- R. Because by Your holy Cross You have redeemed the world.

"And when they came to the place which is called The Skull, there they crucified him, and the criminals, one on the right and one on the left" (Lk 23:33).

Often the Romans merely tied their victims to crosses, leaving them there until they died. Jesus, however, was brutally nailed to His. The nails — huge spikes, really — shattered the bones of His hands

– The Eleventh Station –   73

and feet, causing unimaginable pain. His every movement and every breath enormously increased His agony as the nails ate into His flesh and spilled His blood onto the ground below. When we reject God, we reject all goodness: no cruelty remains out of bounds — no horror remains impossible. Yet St. Cyril of Jerusalem reminds us that the God we have rejected still has the power to bring new life out of even the most evil of human acts:

> He stretched out his hands on the cross to encompass the ends of the world. For the central point of the earth is Golgotha.... He who set the sky in place with his spiritual hands stretched out human hands. They were fastened with nails for this purpose: that when the humanity which bore the sins of mankind had been fastened to the wood and died, sin might die with

it, and we might rise again in righteousness. For since death came through one man, life too comes through one man (cf. Rom 5:12-18), the one man as savior voluntarily accepts death. Remember what he said: "I have power to lay down my life, and I have power to take it up again" (Jn 10:18). (*Catechesis 13*)

Prayer

My Jesus, You stretched out Your arms on the cross to embrace all mankind. Yet so often I embrace the very cruelty that drove the nails into Your hands and feet. Forgive me, my Lord, for forgetting the pain and agony You endured for me — for ignoring the pain and agony of those I encounter. Give me the grace never to wound another; never let me drive a nail into tender flesh again. Amen.

†

– THE TWELFTH STATION –

Jesus Dies on the Cross

St. Augustine

St. Augustine, among the greatest of theologians, was born in North Africa in 354 to a pagan father and a Christian mother. His early years were far from promising; as a young man he was clearly more concerned with life's sensual pleasures than with anything spiritual. And when religion finally entered his life, it did so in the form of Manichaeism, a heresy that combined paganism and Gnosticism. Despite this, his mother, St. Monica, prayed unrelentingly for her son's conversion, which finally happened when he was in his early thirties. Augustine was transformed, leaving both his licentiousness and heretical leanings behind. Consecrated bishop of Hippo in North Africa in 395, he valiantly fought Pelagianism, a heresy that threatened to destroy the Church. One of the most penetrating theologians in history, Augustine has left behind voluminous writings, including his *Confessions*, considered one of the great books of Western civilization. He died in 430 and was declared a Doctor of the Church in 1295. His feast day is August 28.

V. We adore You, O Christ, and we praise You.
R. Because by Your holy Cross You have redeemed the world.

"And Jesus uttered a loud cry, and breathed his last. And the curtain in the temple was torn in two, from top to bottom" (Mk 15:37-38).

Jesus takes His last tortured breath and the impossible happens: God dies. The cur-

– The Twelfth Station –

tain in the Temple is then violently ripped asunder. That curtain separated the Holy of Holies, the place of God's special dwelling, from everything that was profane. It is as if the very force of God's departure from our bloodthirsty world destroys the curtain. God is gone. The Holy of Holies lies empty — for there can be no holy place in a world that crucifies its creator. As we contemplate Jesus' body, hanging lifeless on the cross, we also contemplate a world made barren and unbearable by the absence of God. But St. Augustine sees far deeper than we do, and he perceives a very different world:

> As they were looking on, so we too gaze on his wounds as he hangs. We see his blood as he dies. We see the price offered by the redeemer, touch the scars of his resurrection. He bows his head, as if to kiss you. His heart is made bare open, as it were, in love to you. His arms are

extended that he may embrace you. His whole body is displayed for your redemption. Ponder how great these things are. Let all this be rightly weighed in your mind: as he was once fixed to the cross in every part of his body for you, so he may now be fixed in every part of your soul. (*On Virginity*)

Prayer

My Jesus, the thought of You hanging lifeless on the cross is more than I can bear, for my faith is weak. I see only Your broken body, Your blood upon the ground. I can find only death in Your cross, only absence, and I am torn in two. Give me the grace, I pray, to see beyond all that, to know that You are limitless life, that nothing I do can destroy You or Your love. Let the life You have given for me be fixed in every part of my soul, in every part of my being. Be near to me, Lord Jesus; dwell within me. Amen.

†

– THE THIRTEENTH STATION –

Jesus Is Taken Down from the Cross

St. Catherine of Siena

Born in 1347, Catherine was one of a pair of twins, the other of whom died soon after birth. When Catherine was sixteen years old, an elder sister died as well, and her parents attempted to arrange a marriage between Catherine and her sister's widower — but she had other ideas. Cutting off her hair to make herself less attractive, she fasted until her parents relented. Determined to dedicate herself to Christ, she joined the Third Order of St. Dominic and cared for the sick. Catherine was fearless. The papacy had been in exile in Avignon, France, for seventy years until she visited Pope Gregory XI, persuading him to return to Rome. Later, two men claimed the papacy: Urban VI and Clement VII. Catherine worked tirelessly to ensure that the true pope (Urban) would be recognized by the whole Church. Although very involved in Church politics, Catherine was at heart a mystic who wrote moving accounts of her spiritual experiences as well as much sound spiritual advice. She died in 1380 at the age of thirty-three, was canonized in 1461, and was named a Doctor of the Church in 1970. Her feast day is April 29.

> **V.** We adore You, O Christ, and we praise You.
> **R.** Because by Your holy Cross You have redeemed the world.

– The Thirteenth Station –

"Though he was in the form of God, [Jesus] did not count equality with God a thing to be grasped, but emptied himself, taking the form of a servant, being born in the likeness of men. And being found in human form he humbled himself and became obedient unto death, even death on a cross" (Phil 2:6-8).

It is finished. The struggle of life to resist death has run its course. The sounds of a man in agony have dissipated in the hot, dry breeze, and the sobs of the inconsolable woman standing beneath the cross are no longer heard. The one to whom she gave birth has died; all that remains for her is to cradle His lifeless body in her arms one last time. She watches, wincing each time a bloody nail is pulled from His body, but she does not avert her eyes. The cries for blood have come to an end; their makers depart in search of other sport. Imagine those who stood on Golgotha's heights that day. As Christ's broken body was taken down from the cross, could they have denied that death reigned unchallenged? How difficult it is even for us to realize that all was as it must be on that day, for as a lifeless body is taken down from a cross the birth of a new world begins. A single death overthrows all death, and the woman for whom nothing remains becomes a queen. St Catherine of Siena sees this clearly. She rejoices as Jesus is taken down from the cross just as she does on Easter morning:

> By His death He has given us life.
> By enduring insult and abuse He
> has restored our dignity. With His
> hands nailed fast to the cross He
> has freed us from the shackles of
> sin. With His pierced heart He has
> done away with all our hardheart-
> edness. In His being stripped He
> has clothed us. With His blood
> He gives us a bracing drink. With
> His wisdom He has overcome

– The Thirteenth Station –

the devil's malice. By His scourging He has conquered our flesh. In His humble acceptance of disgrace He has vanquished the world's enticements and pride. He has washed us with His overflowing blood. (Letter T28 to Bernabo Visconti, *Catherine of Siena: An Anthology, Volume I*)

Prayer

My Jesus, all was utter stillness as You were taken down from the cross and laid in the arms of Your mother. The whole universe held its breath — for what use is breath or even life itself without You? Give me the grace to wait for You in stillness while You set captives free. Give the world the grace to wait for You in stillness as we yearn for Easter dawn. Amen.

✝

– THE FOURTEENTH STATION –

Jesus Is Laid in the Tomb

St. Teresa of Calcutta

Who doesn't know Mother Teresa? She has become for us a symbol of God's love active in the world. An ethnic Albanian, Anjezë Gonhxe Bojaxhiu was born in 1910 in Skopje, which is today the capital of Macedonia, but at the time was part of the Ottoman Empire. At the age of eighteen she entered the Sisters of Loreto, taking Teresa as her religious name. Sent to India to teach, she was profoundly moved by the poverty she encountered there. In

1946, Sister Teresa had a mystical experience focused on Christ's thirst for souls, and this changed her forever. She left her community in 1948 and founded the Missionaries of Charity to serve the poorest of the poor. Mother Teresa spent the rest of her life in the service of those for whom no one cared — the rejected, the forgotten, the unborn, the dying. She worked tirelessly for them until her last days. Today more than four thousand Missionaries of Charity are spread throughout the globe, and they continue her work. Awarded the Nobel Peace Prize in 1979, Mother Teresa died in 1997. She was canonized in 2016, and her feast day is September 5.

> V. We adore You, O Christ, and we praise You.
> R. Because by Your holy Cross You have redeemed the world.

– The Fourteenth Station – 87

"When it was evening, there came a rich man from Arimathea, named Joseph, who also was a disciple of Jesus. He went to Pilate and asked for the body of Jesus. Then Pilate ordered it to be given to him. And Joseph took the body, and wrapped it in a clean linen shroud, and laid it in his own new tomb, which he had hewn in the rock; and he rolled a great stone to the door of the tomb, and departed" (Mt 27:57-60).

The players depart the stage, for the struggle of light against darkness seems over, and the winner is obvious. Yet there remains another scene, one no dramatist would have included. A man called Joseph begs for the body of Jesus. Tenderly, he wraps it in clean linen and lays it in his own tomb, surrendering his final resting place to another. A heavy stone then seals the tomb, and Jesus is swallowed up in darkness. Yet *all* is not dark, for Joseph's is an act of light. In His crucifixion and death

Jesus' poverty becomes perfect. Everything has been taken from Him. He hasn't even a place to be buried. Yet the love He bears into the world is alive in Joseph's generosity! Having been reduced to nothing, the Savior sleeps in the darkness of a borrowed tomb, but as St. Teresa of Calcutta knows, from that poverty endless light will soon shine:

> Our Lord on the cross possessed nothing … He was on the cross that was given by Pilate. The nails and the crown were given by the soldiers. He was naked, and when He died, cross, nails and crown were taken away from Him. He was wrapped in a shroud given by a kind heart, and buried in a tomb that was not His. Yet Jesus could have died as a king, and He could have risen from the dead as a king. He chose poverty because

– The Fourteenth Station –

He knew in His infinite knowledge and wisdom that it is the real means of possessing God, of conquering His heart, of bringing His love down to this earth. (*The Love of Christ: Spiritual Counsels*)

Prayer

My Jesus, Your Way of the Cross is completed, and You rest in darkness. I rejoice, for Your pain is over and the reign of night will soon come to its end. In Your death You become my victorious King, the One for whom I wait in hope. I beg You to give me the grace to empty myself for others as You did. I ask for the strength to embrace Your poverty, a poverty so beautiful that it brings God's love down to this troubled earth. Amen.

✝

– THE FIFTEENTH STATION –

The Resurrection

St. Teresa Benedicta of the Cross
(Edith Stein)

Edith Stein, the youngest child of a large Jewish family in Germany, was born in 1891. Highly intelligent, she was among the few women of her generation to attend a German university. At twenty-four she was immersed in doctoral studies and soon was considered one of the most acute philosophical minds of her generation. Yet for most of her early life she had no sense of God. Having rejected the religion of her birth, Edith Stein was an atheist until she read the autobiography of St. Teresa of Avila, which changed her life. She entered the Church and later became a Carmelite nun. Yet she was denied the serenity of the cloister. The rise of Nazism put Sister Teresa Benedicta at risk because of her Jewish roots. She was transferred to Holland, but this bought only a little time. When the German army overran Holland, Sister Teresa Benedicta was deported to Auschwitz, Poland. She was killed on August 9, 1942, and that day is now her feast day. Canonized in 1998, St. Teresa Benedicta of the Cross is a saint who walked the Way of the Cross in an all-but literal way.

> V. We adore You, O Christ, and we praise You.
> R. Because by Your holy Cross You have redeemed the world.

– The Fifteenth Station – 93

"Why do you seek the living among the dead? He is not here but has risen" (Lk 24:5).

The Way of the Cross seems to lead into ever deeper darkness, into suffering so intense that we doubt we can fully imagine it. Yet this journey, begun by a newborn in Bethlehem and continued by a grown man on Golgotha, is infinitely more than it seems to be. The world tells us that the closing of a tomb and the coming of an endless night mark the inevitable end of such a journey. Yet there is no inevitability with God except that of boundless love. In the Way of the Cross, what the world sees as unavoidable is not just overturned but utterly transformed: darkness becomes light; pain becomes joy; death becomes a life so powerful that it dispels every shadow and obliterates every fear. St. Teresa Benedicta of the Cross teaches us that although there is great pain and suffering in the Way of the Cross, there is no despair, for the Way of the Cross is the way to the Resurrection, the way to joy, the way to our Father in heaven:

> The Christian mysteries are an indivisible whole.... Thus the way from Bethlehem leads inevitably to Golgotha, from the crib to the Cross. [Simeon's] prophecy announced the Passion, the fight between light and darkness that already showed itself before the crib.... The star of Bethlehem shines in the night of sin. The shadow of the Cross falls on the light that shines from the crib. This light is extinguished in the darkness of Good Friday, but it rises all the more brilliantly in the sun of grace on the morning of the Resurrection. The way of the incarnate Son of God leads

through the Cross and Passion to the glory of the Resurrection. In His company the way of every one of us, indeed of all humanity, leads through suffering and death to this same glorious goal. (Lecture: "The Mystery of Christmas")

Prayer
My Jesus, it is the first day of the week, and You discard death as easily as You discard the shroud in which You are wrapped. In brilliant light the Father raises You from Your tomb, and we are blinded by Your glory. You who walked the Way of the Cross now walk among us again, scattering darkness with every step. I praise You, my Lord. Your way of suffering has become my way of joy. You are my light. You are my all. I ask but one thing: Let me never be parted from You. Amen.

Other Books by John Collins

A Friar's Tale: Remembering Fr. Benedict J. Groeschel, CFR

Defender of the outcast, acclaimed teacher and spiritual director, insightful psychologist, and founding member of a thriving religious community — yet at heart Fr. Benedict Groeschel was a simple friar. Here is his inspiring, moving, and sometimes humorous biography that invites readers to immerse themselves in the fascinating details of a remarkable life, one animated by faith and devoted to love. ID# T1702

The Way of the Cross with the Saints, Parish Edition

Each of the Stations of the Cross are accompanied by a saint whose thoughts illuminate the way, revealing light behind the darkness of each moment. Perfect for parishwide use. Bulk discounts available. ID# X1833